Relationships are fragile and, once broken, extremely hard to repair.

Between us we have over 50 years' experience of marriage, raising children and living as single parents coping with separation and divorce.

This book will help you to nurture your relationship at all times: to treat it with respect, to value it, and to give it the best chance of lasting.

COMMON SENSE
for COUPLES

love that lasts

JANE BRIDGE & JOHN KLINCK

DIB
books

Common Sense for Couples
Love that Lasts

Copyright © Jane Bridge & John Klinck, 2014.
All rights reserved

Cover design and interior layout © DIB Books, 2014.
Cover art copyright © Masson, 2014 / Shutterstock.

The thoughts and opinions expressed in this book are the authors' and nobody else's. They come from their own experience and discussions.

ISBN-13: 978-1-78532-000-2
ISBN-10: 1-78532-000-9

Published by DIB Books, 2014.

www.dibbooks.com

COMMON SENSE *for* COUPLES

love that lasts

JANE BRIDGE & JOHN KLINCK

ABOUT THE AUTHORS

Jane Bridge was a family law barrister for many years before changing the direction of her career to become a family mediator. For the last 20 years she has been working with couples who have decided to separate or divorce, helping them to reach agreements about their children and finances. In the course of her work she has heard hundreds of stories from clients about what led to the breakdown of their relationships and what they wish they could have done differently. Over the last 25 years she has co-authored many family law textbooks.

John Klinck is a hospital doctor, with over 30 years' experience of working in the NHS. He has specialised in paediatric anaesthesia and intensive care for organ transplantation, which has brought him into contact with children and adults from all walks of life.

Before they met, both authors had brought up children and been through divorces. Therefore, they have first-hand knowledge of the stresses and strains involved in long-term relationships. Together, they have decided to summarise in this short, informative book what they have learned from their accumulated personal knowledge and experience. They hope to pass on to others some positive ways to nurture and sustain relationships in the hope that the trauma of separation and divorce can be avoided.

ACKNOWLEDGEMENTS

We **would like** to acknowledge the assistance and support of our family and friends who have helped us to bring this book to you: Jane's son, David Bridge, who organised the cover art, edited and published it for us; John and Abigail Harman who read the proofs and made helpful and constructive comments throughout; and David and Caroline Borshoff who cast their expert eyes over the content and encouraged us from start to finish.

COMMON SENSE *for* **COUPLES**

love that lasts

CONTENTS

*The thoughts and opinions
expressed in this book
are our own and nobody else's.*

*They come simply from our
own experience and discussions.*

INTRODUCTION

Why Should You Buy This Book?

Why is this book different from others you may have read concerning relationships? In our experience, typical self-help books are generally about retrieving and restoring the 'self' after the worst has happened in a relationship as opposed to retrieving and restoring the relationship itself. Relationships are fragile and, once broken, extremely hard to repair. This book has been written to help you to nurture your relationship at all times, to treat it with respect and to value it so that you give it the best chance of lasting. Unfortunately, once one or both partners are unhappy and are at the stage of seeking counselling it may already be too late to save the relationship.

Ironically, the biological imperative to pair off happens at a time in your life when you have the poorest tools to sustain it. During your 20's and early 30's your life experience is short and your 'emotional intelligence' is limited. Recognising early the factors that may indicate the risk of relationship breakdown, and addressing them, can help to preserve a healthy relationship. Very few couples naturally possess these tools, but many others can learn to use them to the benefit of their relationship.

We think that this book can be useful at any number of 'trigger' points for potential breakdown, for example;

- ▶ Before the start of a relationship – is this the right person for me?
- ▶ When considering whether or not to move in together
- ▶ When considering whether or not to get engaged
- ▶ When considering whether or not to get married
- ▶ When the 'honeymoon' period is over and reality descends
- ▶ When children are born and the couple have less time for one another
- ▶ During a 'mid-life crisis' when one or both partners are wondering whether this relationship is all that life has to offer
- ▶ When considering whether or not to have an affair
- ▶ When considering whether or not to separate
- ▶ When a parent, close relative or a child dies
- ▶ When one of the partners becomes redundant and / or bankrupt

▶ When there is some other financial crisis or mistrust over spending etc.

Between us we, the authors, have over 30 years' experience of marriage and raising children and a further 20 years of life as single parents coping with separation and divorce. We have been lucky enough to find a new relationship together. As a result of what we have been through we realise how precious that is and we are determined to look after it to the best of our ability. We would like to share with you what we have learned in the hope that it may be of some help to you in enhancing your own relationship. If we could sum up in one sentence the goal that this book is intended to achieve, it would be 'an ounce of prevention is worth a pound of cure'.

CHAPTER ONE

How Healthy Is Your Relationship:
Is It Worth Saving?

B**efore** you go any further, take a few minutes to answer this simple questionnaire.

Questionnaire:

▶ Do you like your partner?

▶ Do you respect your partner?

▶ Do you enjoy spending time in your partner's company?

▶ Do you have a satisfying sex life with your partner?

▶ Do you have shared interests with your partner?

▶ Do you have some separate hobbies, interests or pastimes that each of you feels free to pursue without upsetting the other person?

▶ Do you like some of your partner's friends?

▶ Do you discuss your finances together at least once per year?

▶ Have you always been faithful to your partner?

- ▶ Do you get on with your partner's family?
- ▶ Does your partner get on with your family?
- ▶ Do you share the household chores with your partner?
- ▶ Do you and your partner eat most of your evening meals together?
- ▶ Do you talk to your partner openly about how you feel?
- ▶ Does your partner talk to you openly about he/she feels?
- ▶ Do you have friends you can talk to about your relationship?
- ▶ Do you find it easy to agree with your partner about where to go on holiday?
- ▶ Do you know the legal consequences of separating?

If you also have children:

- ▶ Do you allow someone else to mind / babysit your children at least once per week so that you can have some time together as a couple?
- ▶ Do you go away for the weekend without your children sometimes?
- ▶ Do you go on holiday without your children sometimes?

Results:

If your answers were mainly 'No' then this book may be unlikely to help you with your relationship! Turn to Chapter 13 for some useful ideas about how to move forward. If at least half of your answers were 'Yes' then you may find some suggestions in the rest of this book to enhance your relationship.

CHAPTER TWO

*Can Men And Women Ever Live
Together Happily?*

The **truth** of the matter is that men and women are 'wired' differently in terms of their roles, values and expectations. There is a plethora of books explaining the differences between male and female psychology, amongst which we have found John Gray's book *Men are from Mars, Women are from Venus* (Harper Collins Publishers Limited) and Deborah Tannen's book *You Just Don't Understand, Women and Men in Conversation* (Virago Press Limited) extraordinarily helpful. A list of recommended reading is to be found at the end of this book.

Falling in love is an exciting, heady time when life together is comparatively easy because ego boundaries are eroded, you make massive efforts to please one another and obstacles seem insignificant in comparison with the enormity and strength of your immediate emotions. However, once the 'honeymoon' period is over real life sets in, ego boundaries are restored (in whole, or in part) and the true test of the longevity of the relationship begins. M Scott

Peck's book *The Road Less Travelled* (Rider, Ebury Press, Random House) has a wonderful section on 'Love' that tackles the whole subject in detail.

The way that you choose a partner is affected by an infinite number of factors and influences. The importance of your childhood experiences, your role models and your position in the family cannot be underestimated in relation to your choice of partner. Sometimes we choose 'unsuitable' partners for subconscious reasons. Often it is not until later in life that we understand this. A wonderful book to read on this subject is *Families and How to Survive Them* by John Cleese and Robin Skinner. For a relationship to be successful you first need to have some understanding of yourself and how your perception of yourself will be affected by being in a couple relationship. It is trite to say that 'you can't make someone love you', but no less true for that. Often people enter into relationships based on a superficial physical and / or sexual attraction thinking that they can mould or change the other person into someone more 'suitable' to their own ideals; this is usually a recipe for disaster.

Some essential ingredients

Equality

It has been our experience that unless there is true equality between the partners in most areas the relationship is unlikely to last long-term. It is vital that you love, like and respect one another; it is possible to experience one or two of these feelings at the same time but less usual to experience all three together. It is important that you have shared values - emotional, family, children, material, financial, professional, integrity / honesty, hard work, recreation etc. (See Chapter 3)

Sexual compatibility

This is the 'glue' that holds a couple together when everything else may be disintegrating around them. If there is sexual incompatibility then over the course of time it is highly likely that one or both partners will become despondent, frustrated and unhappy. Maintaining and preserving sexual intimacy, a secret garden protected from other people, is a vital part of any successful relationship. (See Chapter 5).

Open communication

Being able to talk to one another about anything and everything means that many problems can be exposed and dealt with before they become a danger to the relationship. Conversely, if one person feels that there are certain subjects that they simply cannot raise with their partner because of their possible reaction then resentment is likely to fester under the surface and erupt at some point. (See Chapter 4).

The ability to compromise

This is another vital skill for anyone wishing to preserve their relationship. Holding out for what you want or what you see as 'right' is often not as important as being able to compromise your wishes and accept that sometimes it is better to allow the other person's perception of what is 'right' to hold sway, even if you think that they are wrong! (See Chapter 4).

Being of a similar age

There are, of course, many successful relationships in which the partners concerned are of very different ages. However, as a general rule, partners who are of the same generation have more in common than those who are not and are therefore more likely to have experienced shared cultural influences as they have grown up e.g. parents who are now in the same age group, similar opportunities for education, exposure to the same types of music, television and fashion and so forth. (See Chapter 3).

Shared projects / hobbies / activities / sports

It is vital to any successful relationship that partners have some shared interests outside their immediate home and family. These will provide opportunities for them to spend quality time together and to have something different and interesting to talk about. Devoting time to a shared project or activity is an excellent way of putting everyday worries into perspective and escaping from domestic frustrations. (See Chapter 3).

Children

It is crucial that partners discuss openly and honestly the possibility of having children. If one partner is desperate to have them and the other is not, then this is likely to become a 'make or break' issue for the relationship sooner or later. (See Chapter 6)

We explore each of the above topics, and many more, in greater detail in the following chapters.

CHAPTER THREE

Compatibility

As we have already touched on in Chapter 2, the superficial characteristics that initially attract you to someone may disguise inner qualities in them which turn out to be fundamentally incompatible with your own personality. Sometimes people have invested so much emotionally in a relationship by the time they discover this that it seems easier to carry on trying to make things work than to step back and consider whether it would be better for both of you to separate. Continuing in a relationship which does not make you happy means that you also give up the possibility of meeting someone new.

Equality

It has been our experience that unless there is true equality between the partners in most areas the relationship is unlikely to last long-term. It is vital that you love, like and respect one another; it is possible to experience one or two of these feelings at the same time but less usual to experience all three together. It is important that you have shared values, for example in relation to your emotional life, your families, your children, your material circumstances, your financial aims and aspirations, your professional lives and careers, your recreational pursuits and your views about integrity, honesty, hard work and so forth.

It is also important that each of you brings to the relationship qualities and characteristics that balance the dynamics between you. For example, you may both have careers but one of you may spend more time outside the home earning money whilst the other combines their paid job with caring for the home and / or children or elderly relatives. From an objective standpoint each role may be valuable in itself, but the crunch question is whether each partner *perceives* his/her role to be of equal value to that of the other.

Respect for one another

It is vital that each partner has, or earns, the respect of the other and this does not necessarily mean respect for one another's natural talents, appearance, skills, achievements and so on. In reality, it is about the effort that each puts into the relationship. Of course, each person has a different perception as to what constitutes 'effort' and it is important that the couple have similar criteria for this. If, for example, the main breadwinner uses financial criteria to judge effort then he/she may feel that they are putting more effort into the relationship than the partner who spends more time at home caring for the house and family rather than bringing in income.

Laziness is the 'root of all evil' and may well lead to the slow death of a relationship. If one partner carries more than their fair share of the responsibilities and realises as time goes by that the other is simply not prepared to pull their weight, then this needs to be addressed openly.

Story

Ann and Dean both had full-time jobs outside the home. However, Ann shouldered the vast majority of the work inside the home, caring for their two children aged 12 and 10 and taking care of the household bills as well as making regular visits to Dean's elderly mother who lived in a care home. Ann often asked Dean to help out but he continued to spend a lot of time at the local pub after work during the week and played golf regularly at the weekends. After 15 years of marriage Ann told Dean that she wanted a divorce as she felt that her efforts were undervalued by him and she had come to the realisation that he was unlikely to change. Dean was shocked at this and offered to enter couples counselling with Ann to tackle the problem. With the help of their counsellor Ann was able to explain how she felt and Dean finally understood that unless he carried his share of the family responsibilities the marriage would be at an end.

Compromise is in itself a form of effort since one person has to agree to sacrifice something in order to please the other. In the example above, Dean would have to agree to sacrifice some of his time at the pub and playing golf in order to be able to take on some of the family responsibilities. In return, Ann would have to agree to put aside her anger at Dean in order to give him sufficient opportunity to show that he could help her.

Having respect for one another includes not 'putting down' the other person, especially in the presence of friends. Negative, critical comments made frequently over a long period of time may well erode the relationship, perhaps irretrievably.

Story

When Sue and Mark were out with their close friends, Sue would routinely criticise Mark for spending too much time at work and never being available to take her out or to take their three children aged 10, 8 and 6 to their various activities. She would take every opportunity to make snide remarks. This was upsetting for Mark and he tried to ignore it or to laugh it off as he was aware that it was very uncomfortable for other people to listen to. Mark felt that he carried all the financial responsibility for the family as Sue did not work. He did not feel that her criticisms were deserved. The more he ignored the criticisms, the more frustrated Sue became and the more frequently and loudly she complained – in private and in public. Eventually, Mark had had enough. He had an affair with a younger woman at work and told Sue he was leaving her. Sue was shocked and upset and suggested marital counselling to try to repair the relationship. With the help of the counsellor Sue was able to explain how neglected she felt and Mark was able to explain how upsetting it was to hear constant negativity from her and how responsible he felt for the family finances. They were able to arrange to go out on a 'date' together once a week and Mark explained that although he was not able to help much with the children during the week, he would take more responsibility for them at the weekend.

Happy couples routinely say appreciative things to one another – thanking the other person for help with household tasks, telling them they look attractive, congratulating them on successes and promotions, doing kind things for one another without being asked, arranging unexpected outings as a surprise, remembering birthdays and anniversaries, reversing roles from time to time so that a job which is habitually done by one of them is done by the other and so on. Getting into the habit of affirming the positive means that the small things that irritate one about the other diminish over time when viewed against all the compensating qualities. Furthermore, other people like to be around couples who are good to one another and who obviously like each other! It promotes a happy environment for everyone.

Preserving the ego boundaries after the first flush of romance

After the heady early days of the relationship in which a couple wish to be together all the time, it is important that they start to build in agreements about how to spend some time apart pursuing their own interests, and how to enable one another to see separate friends and family. This is always a tricky negotiation because when one partner suggests separate time, the other may feel that it is because they are no longer interesting or attractive enough. In reality, the very fact of having some time apart is often a strengthening factor for a long-term relationship, as it allows each person to retain some sense of their own autonomy and individuality in parallel with 'coupledom'.

Age

As a general rule, partners who are of the same genera-tion are likely to have more in common than those who are not and are likely to have experienced shared cultural influences as they have grown up.

However, where there is a big age gap between partners it is likely that they have been born in different genera-tions, exposed to many differences in styles of parenting, education, culture, work patterns, music, fashion, sport, health regimes, social mores and so on. Whilst these dif-ferences may not surface during the 'honeymoon' pe-riod, as the relationship progresses through the years it is likely that they will emerge sooner or later and cause tension. The differences may become particularly stark as the older partner approaches retirement and old age, with its accompanying decline in health and energy. The other partner may still be active and healthy and find that their lifestyle and activities are curtailed as a result, lead-ing to feelings of frustration and discontent.

To compensate for this, it is important to find shared interests that the couple can enjoy together. As retirement approaches, it would be wise to plan ahead the way in which the older partner will occupy their time whilst the younger is still working. Easing into retirement by working part-time may make the process less stressful. Considering a regular routine revolving around, for example, sports, hobbies, further education courses and so on may also be helpful.

Shared projects / hobbies / activities / sports

It is vital to any successful relationship that partners have some shared interests outside their immediate home and family. These will provide opportunities for them to spend quality time together and to have something different and interesting to talk about. Devoting time to a shared project or activity is an excellent way of putting everyday worries into perspective and escaping from domestic frustrations.

Socialising with other people / couples

At the start of a relationship the couple will gradually meet one another's friends. It is unlikely that one partner will get on with all of the other person's friends. As a couple it is important to choose your friends wisely and to consider 'rationing time' with those you do not both get along with. It may be worth one partner spending separate time with friends the other really does not like instead of expecting everyone to compromise.

However, there are bound to be times when meeting up with 'difficult' friends cannot be avoided and then the important thing is to plan a strategy for surviving those people who tend to bring negativity into your lives.

Cultural differences

Where partners come from different countries, it is essential that each tries to learn as much as possible about the other person's culture, language, race, religion and so forth. On one hand international partnerships can be incredibly enriching, but on the other there is much potential for misunderstanding if each partner's expectations of what a relationship entails are quite different from those of the other.

Story

Lily is Japanese and James is British. They met at university in London ten years ago, got married and settled down there. They have a son, Riku, who is now aged 6. Their relationship has gradually deteriorated over the last two years. Lily wishes Riku to attend Japanese school every Saturday morning so that he can learn about his maternal culture, whereas James feels strongly that Riku should be able to relax at home at the weekends like his friends. This difference of approach caused many arguments between them and they were unable to resolve it. Lily found herself wishing to return to Japan with Riku. James was horrified at this possibility. Finally, they sought counselling and were able to reach a compromise whereby Riku would attend Japanese school on Saturday mornings during the term time until he was 11. After that, they would allow him to decide whether or not he wished to continue. Lily and James were able to explore in counselling the importance of their own culture and upbringing in relation to their expectations of one another in their relationship, and their aspirations for their son. They agreed that it was important for Riku to be brought up knowing about both sides of his family.

Where partners come from countries that are far apart, particularly if they still have close relatives living in their country of origin, it can be difficult to stay in touch with family. Travelling 'home' may be expensive and therefore trips may be infrequent. If one partner feels too far away from their birth family to seek support, particularly at stressful times, then this can be a source of tension in a relationship. Therefore, it is important for couples to talk about how they can continue to keep in contact with their respective families in spite of the distance. These days there are many ways of staying in touch by email, Skype, cheap-rate telephone calls and so on.

Top Tips for compatibility

▶ Preserve equality between you

▶ Balance financial responsibility with responsibility for the home and children

▶ Appreciate one another's qualities and contributions at all times, and say so

▶ Affirm the positive things about one another

▶ Continue to work hard to earn one another's respect throughout the relationship

▶ Take time to find out about one another's culture and upbringing, and how this might affect your expectations of one another

▶ Develop the art of compromise – is it always important to be 'right'?

▶ Never 'put down' the other person, particularly in public

▶ Build in separate time and separate friends for each of you

▶ Make time to participate together in shared interests and hobbies

▶ Arrange to go out on 'dates' together regularly

▶ Choose to socialise with other friends / couples who have a positive outlook on life

▶ Use every form of communication open to you when staying in touch with your support network of family and friends, including email, Facebook, Twitter, Skype, cheap-rate international phone calls etc.

CHAPTER FOUR

Communication

Open communication

Being able to talk to one another about anything and everything means that many problems can be exposed and dealt with before they become a danger to the relationship. Conversely, if one person feels that there are certain subjects that they simply cannot raise with their partner because of their possible reaction then resentment is likely to fester under the surface and erupt at some point.

How not to communicate...

- ▶ Don't try to start a conversation when you are both stressed, busy, tired or hungry – it will simply add fuel to the fire
- ▶ Don't start a conversation when either of you has been drinking alcohol
- ▶ Don't use attacking, blaming language – it will only result in an upward spiral of aggression
- ▶ Don't choose a time to talk when there are children or others around – they will feel uncomfortable and may even feel they have to take sides
- ▶ Don't say things that you do not really mean - once they are 'out there' you cannot take them back
- ▶ Don't put things in writing without thinking through the consequences - saying things you later regret is bad enough, but committing words to paper by email, letter, fax or text message may be even worse; they can be printed out and used against you later
- ▶ Think before you press the 'send' button!
- ▶ Words are powerful – mind how you use them!

How to communicate in a positive way

- ▶ Be careful how you start the conversation, as this will colour the way that it continues

- ▶ Choose the right time and place to talk. If possible, agree a time and place to sit down quietly together when there is no-one else about and there are no distractions.

- ▶ Make sure you are both sober

- ▶ Make sure that you are both as calm as possible and that you have had something to eat. It can be hard to keep things in perspective and to stay in control of what you say when your energy and blood sugar levels are not at their best

- ▶ Try to put yourself in the other person's shoes and consider what it would feel like to be on the receiving end of what you are saying

- ▶ Be prepared to listen to, and sometimes even to agree with, criticism of yourself - you might learn something about yourself that you may not have realised before

- ▶ Be prepared to be 'wrong' sometimes – it may be important to allow the other person to be 'right' from time to time

► Start the conversation using 'open' non-blaming language, rather than using words that imply criticism or blame. If the other person feels that they are being accused of doing something wrong they are likely to feel defensive and start to justify their position, rather than listening to what you say

► Consider using 'I' statements that describe how you feel, rather than blaming the other person by using statements that begin with 'you'

Example

Don't say: 'You are always putting me down in front of our friends, you know I hate it!'

Instead try: 'It makes me feel upset when you criticise me in front of our friends'

► When asking the other person to do something, using the right words and being direct can make a huge difference. For example, saying 'Would you be kind enough to hang out the washing?' is much more likely to result in co-operation than saying 'Could you *please* hang out the washing - I've been busy doing all the chores whilst all you have done is watch TV!'

► The use of 'open' questions implies curiosity about how the other person feels, and is much more likely to move the conversation forward in a constructive way

For example, try:

- *How would you feel if…?*
- *What do you think might help?*
- *What are your thoughts about…?*
- *How do you see….?*

The ability to compromise

Holding out for what you want or for what you think is 'right' is often not as important as being able to compromise your wishes and accept that sometimes it is better to allow the other person's perception of what is 'right' to hold sway (even if you think that they are wrong!).

Practise being prepared to take a step back over issues that are not all that important in the greater scheme of things. It can be helpful to ask yourself: 'Will this really matter in a year's time?'

If not, then can you just let it go?

What happens when communication breaks down?

Story

Maggie and Henry have been married for 15 years. Their two children are aged 14 and 8. Henry is an Army officer and has spent long periods of time on active service abroad during the marriage. Maggie is a part-time teacher and feels that she has raised the children more or less on her own. Henry was recently redeployed close to home. He and Maggie now find that they have 'forgotten' how to talk to one another. As a result of his experiences in war zones, Henry is finding it very difficult to talk about his feelings. When Maggie tries to initiate conversations, Henry closes down and withdraws. This makes Maggie feel angry and frustrated, to the point where she sometimes follows him around the house trying to get him to talk to her. This always ends in a row. They realise that they need help to re-establish communication between them. They are having counselling to help them move forward.

They have decided:

▶ To set aside a couple of hours each week to sit down and talk without distractions.

▶ To arrange a babysitter every Friday evening so that they can go out for a meal together

▶ To make sure each of them has equal time to speak without being interrupted

▶ To try to listen respectfully to what the other person has to say, before putting forward their own views

▶ To try to focus on the positive things that they like about one another

▶ To try to be honest with one another about the things they do not like so much, and discuss ways to improve the situation

▶ Henry has also signed up for some one-to-one counselling to help him to work through some of his war-time experiences

Top Tips for better communication

▶ Try to talk as soon as you feel things may be going wrong – don't leave it, or it may be too late

▶ Start conversations in an open, positive, non-blaming way

▶ Talk when you are sober, well-fed, comfortably seated and have privacy

▶ Think about the impact of what you are about to say before you say it

▶ Use 'I' statements rather than 'you' statements

▶ Think about the words you are using in written communications before you commit them to paper or press the 'send' button

▶ Stay calm

▶ Put yourself in the other person's shoes from time to time, to see what it would feel like to be on the receiving end of what you are saying to them

▶ Be prepared to be wrong sometimes

▶ Be prepared to hear criticism of yourself sometimes – you might learn something

▶ Make problems mutual – engage the co-operation of the other person to solve them

▶ Try to use 'would you…' instead of 'could you…' when you ask your partner to do something

▶ Use 'open' questions when possible

▶ Practise the art of compromise

▶ Seek counselling if you feel out of your depth in trying to talk things out between you

CHAPTER FIVE

Your Sexual Relationship

Sexual compatibility

This is the 'glue' that holds a couple together when everything else may be disintegrating around them. If there is sexual incompatibility then over the course of time it is highly likely that one or both partners will become despondent, frustrated and unhappy. Maintaining and preserving sexual intimacy, a secret garden protected from other people, is a vital part of any successful relationship.

Making time for sex amongst the strains and stresses of everyday life can be difficult, but the rewards of doing so are priceless. Arranging to go out for dinner, to the cinema, to listen to music, to dance are wonderful ways to focus on one another and to have an opportunity to remind yourselves how much fun it is to spend time together. Putting work, family and other commitments on one side for an evening provides the opportunity for you to give one another your undivided attention – to really listen, to talk and to go to bed together.

▶ Where there are sexual problems in a relationship the very 'glue' that might otherwise hold it together may be missing

▶ If you have children, it is in their interests to have happy parents. Arrange for a regular babysitter to look after them for an evening so that you can go out and enjoy being a couple

▶ Book weekends away together from time to time, and ask grandparents or relatives to look after the children. If you have friends with children of a similar age, consider offering a reciprocal arrangement

Infidelity

The bond of trust created between a couple through sexual intimacy is fragile and, once broken, rarely capable of true repair. After one partner discovers that the other has been unfaithful, a couple may undergo counselling and / or try to 'paper over the cracks' for a time, but it is likely that whenever they embark on a serious argument the 'affair' will be raised and thrown back into the arena. It will never really be forgotten. Ultimately, it may bring about the demise of the relationship.

▶ If one partner has been unfaithful, they should think very carefully about whether or not they confess it to the other partner; the consequences of disclosure can be fatal to the relationship

▶ If other people know about one partner's affair there is always a danger that it will be exposed at some point, and careful thought needs to be given to this

▶ What may be 'just a fling' to one partner, may be seen as an unacceptable breach of trust to the other

▶ Although it is a gross generalisation, it is nevertheless true that for many men 'just sex' with a third party can be compartmentalised and held separately from their feelings about their long-term partner. On the other hand, for women, sex between their partner and another person can often be seen as an unforgivable betrayal that signals the end of the relationship

▶ Before embarking on an affair it may be wise to weigh the risk of discovery and the likely consequences of that against the excitement of starting a secret relationship with another person

Bisexuality / Homosexuality

One partner may discover during the course of a heterosexual relationship that they are really bisexual or homosexual or unhappy with their biological gender. The result may be that, through no fault of the other person, they simply cannot obtain the sexual fulfilment they crave in their current relationship. This discovery may come when a couple have been together for many years, leading to a complete disintegration of their relationship. The other person is likely to be devastated to discover that they have never been able to sexually satisfy their partner and may feel unattractive and inadequate as a result, believing that somehow they did something wrong.

Story

Ralph and Lea met at university, married and have two daughters who are now aged 8 and 6. After ten years of marriage Lea, at the age of 40, met a much younger woman, Carrie, at work and they fell in love. Lea told Ralph about the affair and asked him to leave the family home, which he did. Carrie moved in with Lea and they set up home together. Lea was excited to discover her 'true' sexuality, and was carried away by the romance of her new relationship. However, the consequences for Ralph were devastating as he questioned his role as a male, as a husband and as a father figure to his daughters. It took him a long time to recover from the breakdown of the relationship and to adjust to the new situation. He is finding it hard to trust any new partners.

A key message for anyone who is not quite sure about their sexual orientation is: if in doubt…wait, gain experience and find out ….before you move in to live with someone.

Past sexual abuse

The past sexual history for each partner is a part and parcel of their relationship. If there are unresolved issues of abuse, it is extremely likely that these will surface sooner or later, like an unexploded bomb.

Story

Marie had been sexually abused by her step-father between the ages of 13 to 15. She had confided in her mother at the time, but her mother had protected her husband instead of believing and supporting Marie. Marie did not reveal the secret to her husband, Terry, for many years. She felt unable to have sex with him, except for the times when their two children were conceived. Terry loved Marie sufficiently to put up with this for nearly 20 years. However, when he reached his early 40's he felt that he wanted more from life as he had become a virtual 'monk'. When he threatened to leave, Marie eventually confided in him about the abuse. He thoroughly supported her and encouraged her to seek help, and to pursue criminal proceedings. Unfortunately, Marie was very reluctant to seek therapy and did not feel she could 'face it'. Terry eventually lost patience with her and left. He felt that Marie did not really love him anymore and that his only chance for happiness was to end the marriage and to try to find a new relationship with someone else.

If you have been the victim of sexual abuse:

▶ Try to talk to someone you trust, and seek help

▶ Don't embark on a new relationship until you have worked through, with expert help, the effect of the abuse on you

▶ When you do feel ready to start a new relationship, seriously consider telling your new partner about your past experiences so that they are aware of what has happened and have more understanding of things that may still be sensitive areas for you

Top tips for a healthy sexual relationship

▶ Make time for sex, no matter what – it is the 'glue' that holds a relationship together over the course of time:

- ○ Make sure that you will not be disturbed
- ○ Turn off the phone
- ○ Put on some music
- ○ Light some candles

▶ Arrange a 'date' night together at least once per week

▶ Arrange a weekend away together whenever you can

▶ When on your date, put aside your commitments to work, children and family so that you can focus on one another

▶ Turn off your mobile phone, or put it on silent

▶ Actively 'listen' to one another – it may be the only time you really do so in the hurly-burly of everyday life

▶ Happy parents mean happy children

▶ Negotiate with a friend or relative to babysit for you regularly

▶ Budget for the cost of a babysitter, if you do not have anyone who will do it for free

▶ Ask your babysitter only to call you in an emergency

CHAPTER SIX

Children

Would you like to have children?

It **is crucial** that partners discuss openly and honestly the possibility of having children. If one partner is desperate to have them and the other is not, then this is likely to become a 'make or break' issue for the relationship sooner or later.

New partners, particularly where the woman is of child-bearing age, need to have this conversation as soon as it looks as though their relationship may become long-term. The failure to do so may mean that there is an 'elephant in the room' colouring the hopes and expectations of one or both partners, whilst neither dares to raise the subject for fear that they will not hear what they want from the other person.

Even when a woman or man says at the outset of a relationship that she / he does not want children, it is entirely possible that her / his feelings may change over the course of time. The biological imperative to reproduce is extremely powerful. Trying to 'hold' someone to a prior agreement not to have children may be impossible, and may even be unfair in the sense that people change as they grow older and what was true for them when they are in their 20's may no longer be true for them in their 30's, 40's and so on.

Unplanned pregnancies

An unexpected pregnancy can provide difficult challenges for a couple. On the one hand, it may be greeted with joy by both partners, but on the other it may be that one or both of them have great reservations about going ahead with it.

It is essential that the couple talk about it as early as possible in the pregnancy, so that all options remain open. If there may be a decision to terminate it, then it is vital that both partners have time to talk to one another about the possibilities, to take proper advice, to seek counselling and to discuss the situation with close family or friends and so on before making a choice.

If there is a decision to proceed to full term, then it is important that the couple discuss openly with one another what this might mean for their relationship. Ultimately, of course, they will not know what it will feel like to be parents until the baby is born. But it might help to consider the 'what ifs…' beforehand to try to prepare as fully as possible for the arrival of their child (see below).

The impact of children on a couple's relationship

The arrival of a child on the scene is a huge turning point for a couple. It is often the case that in the early months following the birth of a baby the mother will concentrate almost exclusively on the child and the father may feel isolated and left out. As the baby grows older the father may become more involved in his day-to-day care, but it is likely that the joint focus of the couple will be on their child rather than on one another.

If the birth of one child is a turning point, the arrival of others will almost certainly consolidate permanent changes in a couple's relationship. Raising children is seriously hard work - physically, emotionally and in every other way.

The danger for the couple is that the dynamics of their own relationship may become overshadowed by their parental roles. For example:

▶ They may start to refer to one another as 'mummy' and 'daddy' rather than using one another's names

▶ They may find that most of their conversations revolve around their children

▶ They may struggle to find suitable babysitters and so give up the effort to go out as a couple

▶ They may be too tired to make love

▶ The cost of raising children may put pressure on their finances, causing one or other, or both, to feel that they have to work longer and harder to meet the increasing expenditure

▶ Grandparents may become over-involved and even 'interfering' and critical of one or both parents

▶ There is a risk that the father (although this is a generalisation in terms of gender, it is a common scenario) may come to feel that work is the one way in which he can retain his own identity in the face of all these changes and spend more and more time developing his career, but at the same time feel guilty that he is not more fully involved at home. There may even be a tendency to overwork because the father gets the message from the mother that a higher income is 'better for the children' as it will help them to afford a better lifestyle in the longer term

Preserving the couple relationship

Generally speaking, it is best for children to be raised in one household with both parents if at all possible. In order for this to happen, the parents need to do whatever is necessary to keep their own relationship intact. This means creating time to be a couple, not just to be mum and dad.

Significance of early role models
— Male / Female

Parents provide their children with early role models in terms of what it means to be a man and what it means to be a woman. In turn, the way in which their child develops will dictate what that child will later look for in a future partner.

We would recommend that all parents read *Families and How to Survive Them* by Robin Skyner and John Cleese (Mandarin).

Stages of emotional development

It is vital for parents to try to ensure that their child pro-gresses in a healthy way through the various stages of emotional and physical development. Missing out any of those stages can have far-reaching consequences for him as he becomes an adult. So it is up to the parents to ensure that the child receives emotional and physical nurturing, proper boundaries, and is encouraged lovingly towards appropriate independence as he grows older. The more balanced the parents can be in participating in the raising of their children, the more likely it is that children will grow up with healthy male / female role models.

Boy-girl psychology

Children learn about their sexual identity from their parents. Girls look to their mothers for a model of femininity, and boys look to their fathers for a model of masculinity. Whereas a girl forms an early attachment with her mother and grows up emulating her, a boy needs help from his mother to detach from his babyhood dependence on her and to form a healthy attachment with his father. In order to complete the process boys also need their fathers to love them and encourage them to develop their masculinity. Although girls need to separate from their mothers too, this entails moving further away from mum rather than having to actively detach from her.

Children need both parents

Children need time with both parents, separately and together, in order to develop into healthy adults. It is important for families to spend time together, but also vital for parents to set aside time to be alone with their children one-to-one if possible.

Top tips for parents

Raising children is exhilarating and exhausting. Consider some of these simple ideas!

► Make time for each parent to spend one-to-one time with each child

► Seek and accept help with child-care from grandparents and other relatives

► If both parents work, then arrange your respective work schedules in a fair way

► Share the household chores between you fairly

► Get the children to help with household chores

► Sort out a budget to cope with the children's expenses

► Agree on the ground-rules for parenting, including:

  ○ *Discipline* – Can you present a united front? What are the boundaries? How do you enforce them? What are the sanctions?

  ○ *Bedtimes* – When? Will it be different for each child?

  ○ *Meals* - What times? Who is going to shop and cook?

○ *Eating patterns* – What do you expect from the children? When are treats allowed?

○ *Pocket money* – Will you give this to your children? If so, how much and how often?

○ *Activities and hobbies* – Which ones will each child do? What do they cost? Who is going to take and collect? Can you share lifts with other families?

○ *Schooling* – Which schools will your children attend? Can both of you go to parent/teacher evenings? Who will help with homework? What are the house rules about homework being done?

○ *Culture and religion* – Do you wish your children to have cultural and / or religious education? Are there religious or cultural differences between you? How can they be resolved? Do the extended family have views that affect you? If so, how will you handle this situation?

○ *Health issues* – Who will take children to the doctor when they are ill? Are there any health conditions for your children that require negotiation between you about the long-term care of your child? Will there be regular hospital appointments? If so, who will attend?

► Work out how best to manage family holidays:

- Can each parent give the other a break sometimes?
- Find activities for the children
- Consider taking along children's friends
- Consider going on holiday with other families with children of similar ages
- Find a babysitter during the holiday so that you can go out together as a couple – after all, it is supposed to be a holiday for you too!

Problem areas

Some of the common problems that crop up in families can be avoided:

▶ Conflict between parents in front of their children can be very damaging for the children

▶ If you have a difference of opinion, don't argue in front of the children – agree to continue the discussion at another time, out of their sight and hearing

▶ Try not to use emotional blackmail between you about the children in order to get your own way. This might arise, for example, where one parent is the main breadwinner for the family and the other spends more time at home with the children. If the home-based parent says something like: 'I know what is best for the children because I spend much more time with them than you do' this is likely to make the other parent feel under-valued, shut out and defensive. It may also lead to a row, or to the other parent simply withdrawing without feeling able to voice their views, thus building up resentment and anger that will eventually erupt

▶ Don't try to shut out the other parent from any of the children's arrangements - the reality is that children generally need full input from both of their parents in order to thrive

Disabled children

Children with disabilities often require a huge input of time, energy and emotion from both parents. Sometimes one or both parents may try to 'block out' the fact that their child has physical or mental problems and remain in denial about them, or feel guilty that they must have 'done something wrong' that makes them responsible for those problems. The result is that there is an added strain on the relationship between the parents. Some of the time and energy which they might otherwise have found for one another is diverted into the care needed by their child, leaving very little to spare. It is not unusual to find at least one of the parents becoming the full-time carer for the child, to the point where their own life revolves around that role to the exclusion of all else. This can lead to the gradual disintegration of the relationship between the couple.

Therefore, it is vital that parents have time for a 'break' from caring for disabled children. It may be possible to:

► Negotiate the provision of respite care through social services; and / or seek assistance from family and friends to help out for a few days from time to time during the year

Having a break together is likely to enable parents to:

► Return to the care of their child with renewed energy; and
► Help them to put the focus back on one another during some much-needed couple time

Step-parenting

If one or both partners already have children from previous relationships then it is vital that they talk about the way that their children will integrate into their new relationship. Being open about possible problems and obstacles means that there is an opportunity to discuss them at an early stage and to consider strategies for managing difficulties before they actually arise.

Involving the children in the process of setting ground-rules for the new household is a good way of enabling them to feel included and less resentful about the introduction of a new adult into their lives.

Story

Becky and Sam have each been married before. Becky has two children from her first marriage, Lizzie (9) and Ben (7), who are based with her during the week but spend alternate weekends with their dad. Sam has one son from his first marriage, Nick (5), who spends alternate weekends with him. When Becky and Sam moved in together they had lots of problems in setting ground-rules for the children, because different rules applied in the children's homes with their other parents. They decided that the best thing to do would be to sit down with the three children and discuss what rules would apply in their house. They asked the children for their ideas. Once they had agreed some family rules they got a big sheet of paper and some coloured pens and the children took turns in writing these down in large letters. Then they pinned the sheet up on the kitchen wall where everyone could see it. This worked really well because everyone felt involved in it.

Co-parenting with ex-partners

Separated or divorced parents who move into new relationships often face big challenges in working out how to co-parent their children with their ex-partner. Much will depend on the level of communication between you and your ex. Where there is reasonable communication then making arrangements for the children may be more straightforward. However, if communication is difficult then it may be hard to work out a co-operative parenting plan.

Top tips for separated parents

▶ Keep communication business-like

▶ Keep communication directly between the two of you – do not involve third parties as this is likely to lead to misunderstandings and difficulties

▶ Verbal communication in person or on the telephone is the most immediate way to exchange information

▶ If verbal communication is too difficult, consider setting out your proposals by email so that they can be printed out and kept, as appropriate

▶ Agree on a way to communicate in an emergency e.g. by mobile phone call or text message

▶ Do not argue in front of the children – all the research shows that being involved in conflict between their parents is damaging for children

▶ Work out between you a routine for sharing time with the children, so that they have plenty of contact with both of you

▶ Hold a diary-planning meeting / phone call at regular intervals to discuss the arrangements for the children

▶ Give plenty of notice about any changes to the plan, so that the other parent is not taken by surprise

▶ Work out well in advance what will happen in school holidays, on the children's birthdays, at Christmas, on special days like Mother's Day and Father's Day etc., so that these occasions are not spoilt by unpleasant arguments

▶ Consider taking your children on holiday, or away for a weekend, on a one-to-one basis. It is rare for a child to have a parent all to themselves, particularly if he has siblings. It is a wonderful way to be able to focus exclusively on your child and build a lasting bond

▶ Depending on the age of your children, consider consulting them about their wishes and feelings. If you do this, let them know that you will take their wishes seriously but that in the end mum and dad will be the ones making the decisions

▶ Let children know that it is fine to have two homes

▶ Let children know that both their parents love them and that this will never change

▶ Let children know that the separation / divorce is not their fault

CHAPTER SEVEN

Money

Financial planning

One of the biggest things that couples can do to help their relationship to run smoothly is to be open about their financial position from the start. It is important to disclose to one another your:

- Income
- Savings
- Property
- Other assets
- Pension provision
- Debts and liabilities

When you move in together, it is important to work out a monthly budget for your expenditure to make sure that you can afford to pay all the bills. It would be useful to review this regularly, say at the end of each year, to make sure that your income and expenditure are balanced. An awareness of one another's spending should help you to avoid sliding into debt. Although this may sound very unromantic, it is likely to set your relationship on a steady path where honesty and transparency about finances become a habit and consequently remove the stress of having to worry about whether or not you are solvent.

You may also find it useful to look ahead, say five years, to discuss the way each of you would like your financial situation to develop. This will help to clarify any similarities or differences you may have in your values, goals and expectations. It is better to be open about your differences at the start. Otherwise, there is a danger that you may start down a financial path that one of you may feel pressured into taking whilst not feeling able to express your reservations in case it upsets the other person. This can build secret resentment that is likely to build over time and erupt in the future. An honest exchange of views at the start may cause short-term arguments, but it may well save you from long-term financial complications.

Cohabitation Agreements

If you are not going to get married you may wish to consider making a Cohabitation Agreement setting out what each of you expects of the other in terms of contribution to joint expenses and so on. It can also set out the arrangements that would be made if you were to split up. An experienced family law solicitor can give you advice about this and help you to draft an appropriate agreement. For further tips about cohabitation see Chapter 12.

Financial independence

Once you have made a plan to cover your joint expenditure, you may wish to agree between you that any remaining money is yours to spend as you wish, free from the scrutiny of your partner. Everyone likes to have a degree of autonomy over their financial affairs, and it is healthy to have some financial independence within a relationship.

Children's expenses

If you have children then it is likely that a large proportion of your budget will be used to cover their expenses. This will include food, clothing, shoes, pocket money, clubs and activities, school meals, school trips, school uniform, sports equipment and so on.

If your children are in private school then the fees may be a large part of your annual expenditure. It will be important to plan ahead to make sure that you can afford to keep your children in their schools for the period that you wish. This may mean making economies in other areas, taking advice about financial planning and so on.

If you would like your children to have the opportunity to go to university, then it is important to factor that into your savings plan. Tertiary education is expensive and will involve the payment of tuition fees, accommodation costs and day-to-day living expenses. Some young people will be expected to work during the vacations in order to help pay for their university education.

If this is what you expect from your children, then it would be wise to sit down with them and explain this clearly, so that they know how to plan their time.

Holidays

Family holidays can be very expensive and it would be wise to plan in advance how much you are prepared to spend each year, so that you can save towards your holiday and enjoy it when the time comes. There is nothing worse that coming home from a relaxing holiday to a stack of unexpectedly high credit card bills that you have to spend the rest of the year paying off.

Financial problems

One of the most common trigger points for the breakdown of a relationship is the existence of financial problems for one or both partners, sometimes exacerbated by alcoholism, drug-taking and / or gambling. Where both partners are aware of the shortage of money each may become watchful of the way in which the other spends. For example, a man may criticise a woman for spending money on magazines and hairdressers, whilst a woman may criticise a man for spending money on beer and betting. This resentment grows as money becomes tighter and can become overwhelming, killing feelings of love and affection for one another.

However, matters may be even worse where one partner is over-spending unbeknownst to the other and then this behaviour is suddenly exposed, perhaps by the arrival on the doormat of a Judgement Summons for unpaid debts, or a threat to repossess the house because the mortgage is in arrears. In these circumstances the dire financial situation is compounded by the realisation by one partner that the other has been deceiving them for what may have been a considerable length of time, possibly for months or even years. This breach of trust can be terminal for the couple's relationship.

Story

Jenny and Dave have been married for ten years and have two children, now aged 11 and 9. Dave had always been financially irresponsible and never disclosed to Jenny what he was earning. He works for his brother and describes himself as 'self-employed'. He has never filed accounts and never paid tax. Jenny works part-time and does her best to contribute to the family finances so as to maintain a home for the children. Then one day a letter arrived that she thought was addressed to her as the label was indistinct. She opened it and discovered a letter addressed to Dave saying that he was being made insolvent. He had already missed a couple of important meetings with the Insolvency Service and was now being taken to court. She was devastated and did not know what to do. All that she had worked hard to achieve seemed to be dissolving, and it looked as though their house might be repossessed. She felt very betrayed by Dave's dishonesty and did not feel that she could ever trust him again.

Top tips for healthy finances

▶ Be open and honest about your income and expenditure from the start

▶ Sit down together and formulate a budget

▶ Review the budget at regular intervals, at least once per year

▶ Consider making a five-year plan

▶ Compare your financial goals and expectations

▶ Consider entering into a Cohabitation Agreement if you are not married

▶ Work out between you what is 'your money' to be spent as you see fit without scrutiny by your partner

▶ Make a clear budget to cover the children's expenses

▶ If you decide to pay school fees, discuss what impact this will have on the remainder of your budget

▶ Plan ahead for the cost of tertiary education

▶ Plan ahead for your family holiday, and budget for it throughout the year

▶ If you get into financial difficulties, tell your partner as soon as possible before things escalate

▶ If you have debts you cannot pay, take advice at the Citizens' Advice Bureau and consider the options for consolidating your debts and making a repayment plan with your creditors

▶ If financial difficulties lead to mistrust between you, consider couples' counselling to help you to talk to one another about the situation

CHAPTER EIGHT

Work

I t is important that each partner has meaningful work that they find stimulating and enjoyable, whether this is caring for the family and the home and / or being the breadwinner. This allows each of you to bring home fresh ideas and stimulating conversation at the end of the day. Sharing the worries and triumphs of everyday life allows a couple to focus on one another and feel valued and appreciated. If possible, it is good to spend some time together at the end of each day over a cup of tea or a glass of wine, just chatting about what has happened. Maybe you could do this whilst cooking the evening meal, or, if you have children, then perhaps you could sit down together after the children have gone to bed.

Taking the time to really listen to one another and to empathise with the things that each of you has experienced fosters intimacy on a daily basis. It is a mistake to believe that you 'don't have time' to talk. Everyone can make time if they wish to do so.

Socialising with work colleagues

Where either or both partners work outside the home then it is likely that there will be times when you socialise as a couple with work colleagues. It is really important that you support one another at these times. It lets each of you know that what the other does for a living is valued and appreciated.

Balancing roles within the home

Regardless of who works in the home or out of the home, it is essential that you discuss how the household chores are to be managed. Even if one of you takes principal responsibility for looking after the family and home, there are still likely to be other jobs that need to be done regularly e.g. mowing the lawn, taking out the rubbish, ferrying the children to their various activities, taking time off work to take children to the doctor or the dentist and so on. It is vital for the health of your relationship that you work out a fair balance of responsibility for these things. If one partner feels that they carry the whole burden without the assistance they would like to have from the other person, this is likely to lead to resentment over the course of time.

If the person who works outside the home literally does not have time to help, then consider seeking paid help to cover the relevant tasks. Discuss how this could be fitted into your budget.

Redundancy

These days, unfortunately, it is not unusual for people to experience redundancy at least once during their working lives. The effects can be financially and emotionally devastating for couples. Not only is there a sudden termination of the income on which they have based their lifestyle up until then, but there can be feelings of uselessness, depression and loss of status for the person to whom it has happened. This may be particularly difficult if they have been employed in the same job for many years. There can be a sudden cut-off from colleagues with whom they have shared a large proportion of their working life, followed by a significant change in their social and support network. This may result in depression, sometimes clinical, for which medical advice should be sought. The other partner may become worn down by the change in roles and lifestyle which follows, to the point where their feelings about the continuation of the relationship alter. They may reach the point where they no longer 'recognise' the other person and question the viability of staying in the relationship.

Story

Harry and Gwen have been married for 25 years, and have two children aged 19 and 17. Harry had been an engineer for the same company for the whole of his working life. Out of the blue the company fell on hard times and had to make him redundant, together with many of his colleagues. Harry was nearly 50 years old and found it very difficult to find another job. He became clinically depressed, was prescribed medication and spent his days at home in front of the TV. Gwen tried to motivate him to re-train and look for different work, but Harry could not, or would not, help himself. Eventually Gwen gave up trying to help him and she left him and went to live with her mother for a time. This was the shock that Harry needed; it acted as a catalyst for him to begin to help himself. He sought help from the Jobcentre and arranged to go on a computer course to update his skills. He also offered to do some voluntary work as a driver for the local hospice. Gwen respected the fact that he was starting to make an effort, and after several weeks she agreed to move back into the house and try to repair their relationship.

Top tips if you are made redundant

If you are made redundant, then you may wish to use this as an opportunity to review what you are looking for from your working life.

► Make it your 'job' to find a job
► Find out what state benefits may be available to you and your family to tide you over your period of unemployment
► Consider some sessions of 'Life Coaching' with someone who is trained to help you to analyse your strengths and weaknesses, and look at ways in which you might make new choices about the sort of work you undertake
► Consider becoming self-employed if you have a skill that lends itself to this. If this is an option, get independent financial advice about how to set up a business, how to keep accurate accounts, what expenses might be set off against your income etc.
► 'Sell yourself' in the most advantageous way. Get help in formulating an up to date curriculum vitae (CV) to

submit with job applications. This is the first thing a potential employer will see, and it sets the scene for the decisions they have to make about whether or not to employ you

▶ Put your name down with recruitment agencies

▶ Use personal contacts from previous jobs to find out whether it would be worth applying again to that company

▶ Accept the moral support offered by your family during this very difficult time

▶ Try not to become disheartened and withdrawn if your applications for jobs do not succeed

▶ Consider doing some regular voluntary work during your period of unemployment. This shows future employers that you have a positive work ethic and can help you to stay optimistic and to feel that you are doing something valuable with your time. It is something constructive to add to your CV, and will be a subject you can talk about confidently in job interviews

▶ Remember to keep talking to your partner about the possibilities open to you

▶ Keep all communication channels open with your family, friends, former work colleagues – you never know where the next job offer might come from!

Retirement

Advances in medical care and improvements in the health of the population mean that there is an increase in life expectancy for men and women. The age at which the State Pension becomes payable for men and women is increasing (see the Pensions Advisory Service website www.pensionsadvisoryservice.org.uk):

- ▶ Between 2010 and 2020 women's retirement ages are increasing to 65.
- ▶ Between 2024 and 2026, retirement ages for men and women are increasing to 66.
- ▶ Between 2034 and 2036, retirement ages for men and women are increasing to 67.
- ▶ Between 2044 and 2046, retirement ages for men and women are increasing to 68.

Some people may continue in paid employment well beyond retirement age, but others may choose to retire early or at the state pension age. Whenever you retire, it is likely to be a period of transition and can come as a huge shock to some.

This can be particularly challenging for couples who retire at different times. The pattern of life for the couple will change substantially, and can bring unexpected pressures and changes in your expectations of one another. In view of this it is important to talk about the retirement beforehand and formulate some plans.

Top tips for preparing for retirement

- ▶ Talk about retirement with your partner
- ▶ Talk about your shared wishes and dreams
- ▶ Talk about your individual wishes and dreams
- ▶ Re-balance the household chores to distribute them fairly between you
- ▶ Consider some sessions with a 'Life Coach' to help you to identify the things you would really like to do and that will give you a sense of purpose and fulfilment
- ▶ Plan ahead to give your days a structure. Once the need to get up in the morning to go to work is no longer there you may feel a bit 'lost' after the initial euphoria caused by breaking free of your work routine has worn off
- ▶ Plan your finances carefully to make sure that you have enough to live on. Obtain independent financial advice if there is anything you are not sure about
- ▶ Update your Wills so that if anything happens to either of you the surviving partner is not left with financial uncertainties to cope with
- ▶ Consider moving home if this would make life easier and cheaper

► Consider moving closer to your children or extended family if it is likely that you will need their support as you grow older

► Set aside a budget for the extra things you would like to do, so that you know how much is available to spend on leisure and recreation

► Look after your health to the very best of your ability

► Eat well

► Take enough exercise. Build this into your daily routine

► Plan future projects to give you a focal point

► If you are worried about how to fill your time – you may consider doing something you have always wanted to do, but never had the time to explore, for example:

   o   Learning a new language
   o   Going to evening classes
   o   Joining the University of the Third Age (U3A)
   o   Joining a film club
   o   Joining a rambling club
   o   Taking up a new sport
   o   Doing some voluntary work

► If you enjoy travelling, consider how much you can afford to spend on this each year and plan some trips that have always been on your 'wish list'

CHAPTER NINE

Health

I t is vital to look after your physical, emotional and mental health not just for your own well-being, but also for the quality of your life as a couple.

Top tips to preserve good health:

- ▶ Eat healthy food
- ▶ Cook together as a couple
- ▶ Take regular exercise, together and separately
- ▶ Support one another in seeking advice at the start of any perceived health problem
- ▶ Give each other time to relax at the end of the working day
- ▶ Take time to unwind after a stressful episode
- ▶ See making time for one another as a way to help your individual emotional health, but also your emotional well-being as a couple

- ▶ Keep under regular review your life-work balance, individually and as a couple
- ▶ Make the best use of your weekends to have a change of routine and / or a change of scene
- ▶ Socialise with friends who make you feel good
- ▶ Take regular holidays

Physical disability or illness of one of the partners

Where one of the partners has, or develops, a physical illness, there can be an intolerable strain on the other partner as they find themselves acting as a 'carer' for their own partner. However much they may love one another, over the course of time this may change the balance in the relationship from its previous equality to the dependency of one upon the other and so may undermine the very basis upon which they were first attracted to one another.

Story

Maria came from Spain and has been partially deaf since birth. She wears hearing aids in both ears and lip reads. She was married to Sam for 15 years and they have two sons who are now aged 12 and 8. During the course of the marriage Sam became increasingly controlling and irritable as he became more and more frustrated by her disability. She felt increasingly vulnerable. Her disability left her feeling isolated and emotionally diminished. Sam complained that she was 'not qualified to do anything'. Eventually Maria left the home, as she was extremely depressed, taking the boys with her. Maria had counselling, regained her confidence and retrained as a teacher. She met a new partner and formed a settled relationship with him. In time, she and Sam were able to share time with the boys quite evenly. In her new relationship, her boyfriend took time to listen to her and to understand how she was feeling, being patient with her hearing problems and helping her to develop strategies to manage her disability.

Top tips for managing the disability or illness of one of the partners

These tips apply whether it is you and / or your partner who suffers from the condition:

▶ As soon as you feel that there is a problem, talk to your partner if you can

▶ If you can't talk to your partner about it, try to confide in someone close to you

▶ Talk to your family doctor about the problems you are experiencing

▶ Explore whether there is any further medical help open to the person with the disability or illness, particularly if the condition is getting worse

▶ Consider seeking counselling for yourself, or jointly, as appropriate

▶ Find out about local support groups where you can share your experiences with others who understand

▶ If there is no local support group, consider starting one

Illness within the extended family

Where one of the partners finds themselves caring for a member of their extended family who is ill they may need to be out of the home for lengthy periods, to the point where they have no time, energy or emotion left to invest in their own couple relationship. There is a serious risk that the partner who is 'left behind' begins to feel isolated and uncared for, to the point where they may believe that there is no point in staying in the relationship.

Top tips for managing illness within the extended family

▶ Make sure that you put your couple relationship first

▶ Make sure that you plan some 'time off' during the weekends so that you can spend time with your partner

▶ Consider whether there are other members of the family who can offer help sometimes

▶ Consider whether you can afford to pay someone to help on a regular basis

▶ Consider whether you can seek government allowances for your role as carer, as this might ease your financial position

▶ Consider whether your local authority can offer help with regular care

▶ Consider whether your local authority can offer 'respite care' to give you a break

▶ Find out whether there are local support groups for other carers in your situation, as it can be a relief to talk about the stresses involved with others who understand them

Depression, personality disorders and mental illness

Where one or both partners suffer from depression, a personality disorder or a mental illness, which remains untreated, it is highly likely that the relationship may not stand the test of time. Of course, there are those relationships where one ostensibly 'healthy' partner needs to be with a partner who has to be 'looked after'. It may be that this relationship of co-dependency may work in certain cases because of the underlying personalities and characteristics of those individuals. However, where one partner enters a relationship believing that the other person is physically and mentally well, only to discover over the course of time that they are not, then huge strains may be placed upon the couple. If treatment is sought and acted upon, then the couple may enter into a joint venture to cure the problem and tackle it together, actually strengthening their relationship in the long-run. However, where the problem is not addressed it is likely that the strain upon the healthy partner will take its toll eventually, so that the deteriorating condition and behaviour of the other will eventually erode the relationship to the point that it cannot be repaired.

Top tips for dealing with mental health problems

These tips apply whether it is you and / or your partner who suffers from the condition:

- ▶ As soon as you spot a problem, seek help
- ▶ Make an appointment with your family doctor
- ▶ Discuss the possibility of appropriate medication
- ▶ If it is a complex problem, ask your GP for a referral to a consultant
- ▶ Seek individual and / or joint counselling, as appropriate
- ▶ Confide in close family and/ or friends so that you do not feel so 'alone'

Alcoholism, drug dependency, gambling, sexual addiction

Dependency and addiction involving alcohol, drugs, gambling and sex are major causes of relationship breakdown. Sometimes one partner enters into a relationship knowing that the other has such a problem, but it is probably more common for this to emerge during the course of the relationship. Unless expert help can be sought, and acted on by the sufferer, it is likely that over the course of time the way in which the addiction or dependency affects them will erode the underlying trust between the partners. Examples of such behaviour may include: lying, physical aggression, verbal abuse, irresponsible behaviour, overspending, involvement in criminal activities and so on. The following two stories illustrate some of these problems.

Story

Matt and Hannah were married for eight years and have two daughters, 6 and 4. During the marriage Matt became addicted to cocaine and alcohol. He made several efforts to conquer his addiction but kept sliding back into it whenever he felt under stress. Throughout the marriage Hannah had been subjected to his dramatic mood swings and his emotionally and verbally abusive behaviour. On occasions he was physically violent to her. Hannah decided she could not continue in the marriage and asked Matt to leave. After the separation Matt and Hannah found it almost impossible to communicate on any level. Hannah felt unable to trust him because he had lied to her so often during the marriage, and made so many promises that he had later broken.

Story

Theo and Maya were married for 18 years and had no children. Theo was a college lecturer and Maya worked for the civil service. During the course of the marriage Theo admitted that he had gambled away at least £50,000, but in reality it was probably much more than this. For years he lied to Maya about their financial situation and destroyed evidence of his finances. Maya was always worried that there would not be enough money to pay bills, do maintenance work to the home or to go on holiday. Theo tried to get help for his addiction but was unable to conquer it. Maya supported him for many years in these attempts but eventually she felt that every shred of trust had been lost and she left. She was exhausted and simply wanted to negotiate a 'clean break' financial settlement with Theo so that she need never again be financially linked with him.

Top tips for dealing with addiction

These tips apply whether it is you and / or your partner who suffers from the condition:

▶ Seek help as soon as a problem comes to light

▶ Speak to your family doctor about the problem and find out what help might be available

▶ Confide in your partner if you can and talk about how to move forward

▶ Confide in close family or friends so that it is not a 'secret'

▶ If your safety, or that of your children, is at risk, seek legal advice immediately

▶ If your financial security is at risk, consider speaking to your solicitor, bank manager, accountant or financial adviser to see what can be done to preserve your financial position

▶ If you have fallen into debt, seek specialist debt advice as there may be steps that can be taken to make arrangements with your creditors to organise repayment of the debts in a way that you can manage

▶ Consider expert counselling

▶ Consider finding a suitable support group

CHAPTER TEN

Holidays

Holidays Together

It is important for couples to make time to take holidays together, and separately if they wish. Holidays together give you time away from the hustle and bustle of everyday life when you can focus on one another and share new experiences. This may be by travelling to places that you have never visited before, or by returning to familiar 'old haunts' that you enjoy. Escape from routine allows you both to recharge your batteries.

If you have children, try planning once per year to go away on holiday (or at least for a long weekend) without them. This can give you a much-needed break from being 'mummy and daddy' and remind you what it feels like to spend time together.

Individual holidays

Couples may find it helpful to take individual holidays sometimes, to build in this type of 'me' time. Separate holidays might be taken on your own or with family or friends. Having space from one another from time to time can help to restore your autonomy for a while. Life as a couple can blur the individual boundaries of each partner over the course of time. Peeling back some of the layers of 'coupledom' and restoring a greater sense of self may be useful sometimes. Returning home after a break may remind you how much you miss your partner.

Of course, it may also have the opposite effect! There has to be substantial degree of trust and security in a relationship for couples to take separate holidays without the person 'left behind' feeling that they are being deliberately shut out and abandoned.

Taking the children on holiday

Holidays can be hard work for parents! If you are planning a family holiday, it is a good idea to make sure that there are activities that suit the age groups of your children. If possible, find places that provide some childcare during the day or in the evenings so that you can have some time together away from the children. Consider taking a friend for each child so that they have someone to play with.

It may be good to go on holiday with another family, or families, with children of similar ages so that you can share the childcare with other parents.

Financial planning

Going on holiday can be an expensive business, particularly if you are taking children. It is important to plan your budget well in advance to make sure that you can afford to go without putting excess strain on the household finances.

Managing expectations

It is important for a couple to talk about what each of them expects from a holiday, and to be honest about the things that they really like to do and those they are not so keen on! Each person may have a very different perception of what is meant by escape, relaxation, adventure and so on. It is only possible to cater for individual needs if you are prepared to discuss it openly.

Story

Graham and Nicola have been together for 11 years and have a son Ben who is 9, and a daughter Ruby who is 7. They live in Yorkshire, close to Graham's family who have a cottage in the Dales that they have owned for three generations. It means a great deal to Graham to take Nicola and the children there every summer for a fortnight, together with his parents. However, this is not Nicola's idea of a break! When she is at the cottage she feels that Graham's mother is always in charge, that she has no say in mealtimes and that there is no privacy. In the early years of the marriage she went along with it to please Graham, but since the children were born she feels that she never has a moment to herself, not even on holiday. When the subject of holidays comes up in conversation this year she finally makes a stand and tells Graham how she really feels. He is completely shocked as he thought that she loved the cottage. However, he takes her worries seriously and after talking about what each of them regards as a 'holiday' they agree that Graham will spend the usual fortnight at the cottage with the children and his parents, that Nicola will be there for the first week, but that she will go away to Ibiza with some girlfriends for the second week for sunshine, rest and relaxation.

Top tips for holidays

- ▶ Agree a holiday budget each year and make this an important component of your financial planning
- ▶ Be honest with one another about your perception of what is meant by a 'holiday'
- ▶ If you have very different expectations of a 'holiday' consider going on separate holidays
- ▶ Take a holiday together as a couple at least once per year
- ▶ Try going to new places, as well as to familiar 'old haunts', as this can be very stimulating
- ▶ If you have children:

  - ○ Make sure there are some childcare arrangements at your holiday destination
  - ○ Make sure there are plenty of activities for them (and for you)
  - ○ Consider taking a friend for each of them
  - ○ Consider going on holiday with other families with children of similar ages
  - ○ Go on holiday without the children at least once per year, and forget that you are 'mummy and daddy' for a while!

CHAPTER ELEVEN

The Extended Family

Importance of good family relationships

Entering into a relationship with your partner also means entering into a relationship with their family, and them with yours. This can be an enriching experience or the reverse. If it is the former, then you are lucky. If it is the latter, then there may be some challenges ahead!

Interference by the extended family

Sometimes the extended family can be a source of friction. If the couple find it difficult to cope with one another's families then it can lead to arguments between them, allegations that the partner's loyalties are with their own family rather than with the couple relationship, tension over attending family occasions and so on. It is important that a couple discusses together how to manage these competing loyalties.

Story

Emma worked part-time in her parents' pub. Bob worked for his father's building firm. The families 'called the shots' about the appropriate salary and working conditions for each of them, and this felt as though they were in control of Emma's and Bob's lives. When he discovered that other employees were being paid more than him for doing less hours Bob finally left his father's firm to work for someone else. This caused a big rift with his family and they have not seen them for the last 18 months. Emma has tried to build bridges by offering to take their two children over to visit Bob's parents, but her efforts have been rebuffed so far. This is a great pity for all of them, but particularly for the children who are growing up without contact with their paternal grandparents.

Ground-rules when grandparents provide childcare

Nearly a third of families in Great Britain, where the mother is in work, rely on informal childcare provision from the child's grandparents (Childhood Wellbeing Research Centre Working Paper No 10, November 2011). If you rely on grandparents to provide child care for your children then it would be a good idea to work out some ground-rules for how this will take place:

- ▶ Which days of the week and for how many hours?
- ▶ Will it include school holidays?
- ▶ Will grandparents be paid for their time?
- ▶ In whose house will childcare take place?
- ▶ Who is to provide the equipment for the children, e.g. pushchairs, cots, toys, special chairs, car-seats etc.?
- ▶ Who decides what the children will eat and when?
- ▶ Who will decide about discipline?

Top tips for managing relationships with the extended family:

▶ If you have good relationships with one another's extended families, foster them as they will add greatly to the quality of your lives

▶ If you have tricky relationships with any of the extended family, discuss it between you as a couple and work out strategies to manage them:

- Discuss it openly between you as a couple
- Don't let the extended family 'divide and rule', that is to say, do not let them create a barrier between you and your partner
- Be quick to spot when your loyalties are being split, and 'nip it in the bud'

▶ Work out strategies to manage time with the extended family. This could include, for example:

- Limiting the amount of time you spend with them each year

o Agreeing between you as a couple which family occasions each year you will attend, and which you will not

o Agreeing between you as a couple on an arrival and departure time when you attend family occasions

o Making sure you agree between you an 'exit strategy' i.e. a good reason to leave a family get-together at a specific time

o Making sure that you have your own transport, so that you retain control over your ability to arrive and depart

o If going on holiday with extended family, consider your own family staying in separate accommodation to the rest of them

o Pay for yourselves, so that you are not 'beholden' to anyone else. Be aware that money can become a source of control!

o If grandparents provide child care for your children, agree a set of ground-rules about the practical arrangements

CHAPTER TWELVE

The Wedding Industry:
Shall We Marry Or Just Live Together?

Getting Married: Who Is It Really For?

The decision about whether to get married or to cohabit is complicated. In this chapter, we look at the industry that has been built around weddings, and the stresses that this can bring for those couples who choose to walk down the aisle, or to marry in a registry office. Same-sex couples who enter into civil partnerships will find that these have virtually the same legal consequences as marriage in terms of children and finances.

At the risk of sounding very unromantic, we also give some tips about how to protect yourself financially in case your marriage or relationship breaks down.

To illustrate some of the competing pressures on couples, let's look at the story of Tracey and Dave:

Story

Tracey (27) and Dave (30) have been living together for four years. Tracey really wants to get married and mentions it almost every day, in one way or another. Lots of her friends are getting married and having children. Dave does not think that getting married is all that important. He feels that it is luxury that can be afforded in the future – after they have saved up to buy a house, car, and put some money in the bank. Tracey interprets this as meaning that he does not love her enough to want to marry her. It has become a source of constant rows between them. Tracey equates marriage with security, albeit subconsciously, and would feel safer having her relationship with Dave formalised in a legal framework, so that he is 'taken off the market' so far as other women are concerned. Dave has seen some of his friends get married and 'settle down', only to find that their lives have become restricted by the expectations of their wives and the responsibilities of caring for children. He suspects that getting married may take the fun out of his relationship with Tracey. However, after long dis-

cussions and much heart-searching Dave finally 'pops the question' and he and Tracey become engaged. From then on the process of planning the wedding becomes the prime focus of their lives, with the families on both sides drawn into the vortex of 'wedding fever'.

Once couples have set the date for their wedding, many start to wonder who they are actually getting married for. The process can seem to take on a life of its own, with parents and extended families on either side becoming involved in the roles, preparations, clothing, guest-list, seating plan, flowers, venue, accommodation, honeymoon and so on. The list is endless. What started out as a celebration of the love of one person for the other gathers momentum until, for some, it can feel like a vehicle careering out of control.

Subtle changes can occur as soon as the ink is dry on the marriage certificate and the honeymoon is over. It can be almost as if acquiring the labels 'husband' and 'wife' bring about a change in the way each person sees themselves. Often it means a change of surname for the woman, an alteration of her identity in terms of how she is described by the outside world. There can be a tendency for each partner to fall into the traditional roles and stereotypes associated with 'being a husband' or 'being a wife' (however unlikely that might have seemed before the wedding). Each person may have certain expectations of the other, based on their own family's models of marriage or maybe based on the patterns they see in their friends' marriages. These expectations may turn out to be wholly unrealistic There is a danger that married couples may quite quickly start to make assumptions about one another, stop making so much effort to please one another, and become lazy about 'looking after' the relationship. We hope that the earlier chapters in this book will help you to avoid many of these pitfalls.

All of these factors may be exacerbated when children arrive on the scene. Couples often become exhausted by the constant demands of parenthood, which leaves them no spare energy to devote to one another, a subject discussed in more detail in Chapter 9.

The cost of getting married

A little bit of research shows that the average cost of getting married can be high!

According to an article in The Telegraph, 22 May 2013, edited by Richard Holt, the 'Average wedding now costs more than £18,000':

'Newlywed couples are now going to ever increasing lengths to recoup costs from the wedding, with one in eight (12 per cent) even admitting selling items bought from their gift lists to generate cash.

More than half of newlyweds (52 per cent) think wedding costs have spiralled out of control, with 12 per cent now in more than £3,000 worth of debt due to the cost of their big day.

The poll of more than 1,000 people married within the last five years, by Sheilas' Wheels home insurance, found that 16 per cent of couples argued at least once a week during the planning process because of their finances.

And one in nine newlyweds (11 per cent) admits they even came close to breaking up due to wedding-related money woes.

The study found one in five (21 per cent) had to take out credit cards and loans to pay for their big day with a further 25 per cent borrowing money from family and friends.

Costs are hitting 25 to 34 year-olds the hardest with one-in-five (20 per cent) having to choose between a wedding or getting that first leg up on the property ladder.

A third (33 per cent) admitted getting into debt to pay for their wedding, while 23 per cent put off getting married due to their strained finances.

Almost one in five (18 per cent) blame the pressure to 'keep up with the Jones' as the main reason for wedding costs snowballing, whilst a third (33 per cent) put it down to their ever-expanding guest list.

Pressure to host a free bar has caused 16 per cent of newlyweds' finances to get out of control, and 19 per cent felt obliged to kit out their bridal party with full regalia even though they could not afford it. And 24 per cent of those polled thought they were overcharged by wedding suppliers with 20 per cent admitting they booked venues or caterers and later regretted it, due to the cost.

*A fifth (20 per cent) even said they were too embar-
rassed to haggle or negotiate.*

*The research revealed that 12 per cent admitted they put
items bought from their gift list on eBay and 10 per cent
admit returning them to the shop.*

*One in nine brides sold their wedding dress online to get
some cash and a further 26 per cent ask for money as a
wedding gift to help with finances – 15 per cent even say
it's specifically to pay off debts.*

*A third of Londoners (33 per cent) took out credit
cards or loans to pay for their big day, compared to just
13 per cent in the South West.*

*Londoners were also the most likely to put off buying a
house because of the cost of their wedding (31 per cent).'*

The website for UK Wedding Belles
(www.ukweddingbelles.com) breaks down the average
cost of a wedding in 2011 like this:

Engagement ring and celebrations (£1,200)
Stationery (£500)

Stag and Hen nights (£280)

Insurance (£120)

The service (£520)

Wedding rings (£650)

Flowers (£750)

Reception décor (£500)

Bride's outfit (£1,500)

Hair and beauty (£180)

Groom's outfit (£200)

Attendants' outfits (£480)

Transport (£520)

Photography (£950)

Videography (£900)

Reception (venue, food & drinks) (£4,030)

Entertainment (£750)

Wedding cake (£400)

Gifts (£175)

Honeymoon & first night hotel (£4,000)

Total: £18,605

The cost of a wedding can place an extraordinary burden on the couple and their families. There can be intense emotional pressure on the parents of the bride and groom to either pay for the whole affair or to 'chip in', often at a time when they are nearing retirement.

For many couples the pressure of the 'credit crunch' that started in 2007 and looks set to continue for some time to come means that they will find it much harder to obtain a mortgage for their first home. Increasingly, they will be expected to pay a substantial deposit before a mortgage lender will agree to make a loan. The cost of the wedding is bound to eat into their savings and deplete the funds available for a deposit.

Marriage and divorce statistics

Records compiled by the Office for National Statistics (ONS) show the long–term picture for weddings in the UK is one of gradual decline, although there has been a small increase each year since 2009. It is not possible to say at this stage whether this is indicative of an end to the long-term decline of marriage between 1972 and 2009 (www.ons.gov.uk). It is interesting to look at some of the statistics relating to marriage, civil partnership, cohabitation, divorce and the dissolution of civil partnerships:

▶ The provisional number of UK marriages in 2011 was 285,390 as compared with a peak of 480,285 in 1972

▶ However, since 2009 the number of marriages has increased gradually each year to 2011

▶ The 2011 statistics for England and Wales show that 164,470 (66%) were first marriages for both partners

▶ The number of 2011 marriages for England and Wales was greatest between men and women aged 25 to 29

▶ The number of civil partnerships formed in England and Wales by same-sex couples rose in 2011, increasing to 6,152 compared with 5,804 in 2010 (an increase of 6%).

▶ The mean age of men forming a civil partnership in the UK in 2011 was 40.1 years, while for women the average age was 38.3 years

By way of contrast:

▶ Between 2010 and 2011, the number of divorces granted in the UK fell by 1.7% from 119,589 to 117,558. This continues the general decline in divorces since 2003 when there were 153,065. The fall in divorces is consistent with a decline in the number of marriages to 2009. It may be due to the increasing number of couples choosing to cohabit rather than enter into marriage (Beaujouan and Bhrolchain, 2011).

▶ The number of divorces in 2011 was highest among men and women aged 40 to 44

▶ Based on marriage, divorce and mortality statistics for England and Wales for 2010, it is estimated that the percentage of marriages ending in divorce is 42%. Around half of these divorces occur in the first ten years of marriage

▶ The median duration of marriage (i.e. the mid-point of distribution) for divorces granted in 2011 was 11.5 years.

▶ In 2011, 70% of divorces were to couples where both parties were in their first marriage, while the remaining 30% were to couples where at least one of the parties had been divorced or widowed previously

▶ Almost half (49%) of couples divorcing in 2011 had at least one child aged under 16 living in the family. Over a fifth of the children were under five and 64% were under 11.

▶ The provisional number of civil partnership dissolutions granted in the UK in 2011 was 672, an increase of 28.7 per cent since 2010.

Pre-Nuptial Agreements

As we have seen, more than 40% of UK marriages now end in divorce. When a marriage breaks down, the legal framework regulating divorce is set out in the Matrimonial Causes Act 1973. Any issues concerning the children will be dealt with under the Children Act 1989, and child support problems are largely considered under the Child Support Act 1991.

Although it may not seem very romantic, it is becoming much more common these days for those intending to marry to consider entering into a Pre-nuptial Agreement, particularly where one or both partners has been married before. It sets out the arrangements that will follow if you later decide to separate or divorce. Although such agreements are yet not legally enforceable as such in the UK, courts do place increasingly more weight on them.

A Pre-nuptial Agreement may be particularly appropriate where, for example:

- Either or both of you have been married before
- You are bringing financial assets into the marriage
- There is an inequality of earning power between you
- You are giving up a source of income in order to get married
- You are giving up a home in order to get married

If you think that such an agreement would be a good idea, make sure that you each consult independent solicitors in order to have it drawn up properly. Your solicitors will make sure that you do not sign anything until you have each given one another full details of all your finances, and are happy with the arrangements that you are entering into.

Is there an alternative to marriage?

The Office for National Statistics (www.ons.gov.uk) explains that cohabitation refers to living with a partner, but not married to or in a civil partnership with them. In 2012 there were 5.9 million people cohabiting in the UK, double the 1996 figure. Cohabitation is the fastest growing family type in the UK. In 2006, 58% of respondents to the British Social Attitudes Survey thought that unmarried couples who live together for some time probably or definitely had a 'common law marriage' that gives them the same legal rights as married couples; unfortunately, this is not the case as there is no such thing as 'common law marriage' in UK law.

- ► 25 – 34 year olds are the age group most likely to cohabit, often living together before getting married
- ► The percentage of those in the 35 – 44 year age group who are cohabiting has also increased
- ► Four-fifths of people marrying were living together before their marriage

▶ The percentage of same sex cohabiting couples has increased from 16,000 in 1996 to 69,000 in 2012 (a 345% increase!), whilst the percentage of opposite sex cohabiting couples has increased from 1.46 million in 1996 to 2.84 million in 2012 (a 98% increase)

▶ In 2012, 39% of opposite sex cohabiting couples had dependent children, compared with 38% of married couples. However, less than 1% of dependent children lived in civil partner or same sex cohabiting couple families in 2012.

Cohabitation

If indeed marriage is on the decline and more people are choosing to live together instead, then what practical arrangements can couples make to regulate the basis on which they choose to run their lives? In practice, families come in all shapes and forms, but there are some practical tips for regulating those arrangements.

Top tips for cohabitees

▶ In the early stages of a relationship keep separate homes, at least until you are more certain about the future

▶ If cohabiting couples decide to split up, the law relating to how their financial assets are to be divided between them is very complicated. This means that it can be very expensive and stressful to try to untangle things. Although this may sound very unromantic, there are some sensible steps you can take to protect yourself in case you split up. From the start of your relationship you should:

  ○ Keep clear records of all the financial transactions between you

  ○ Decide who is to pay which bills, and when

  ○ Make written (and dated) agreements about any important financial decisions that you have made

  ○ Record any loans between you in writing (with dates)

  ○ Make it very clear if something is a gift, rather than a loan

- o Keep copies of all your bank statements
- o Keep copies of all your receipts

▶ If you decide to live together, consider consulting separate lawyers and formulating a Cohabitation Agreement. This can cover a wide range of agreements between you to make it clear what each of you expects of the other, and to set out what would happen if you split up

▶ If you decide to rent a property together, make a clear financial agreement about who is to pay for what, and when

▶ If you decide to buy a property together, each partner should take independent legal advice about the appropriate legal framework for the purchase

- o Are you going to purchase the property as joint tenants? If so, the presumption will be that you own it in equal shares, 50:50. Furthermore, if one of you dies, that person's share would pass by the right of 'survivorship' to the remaining partner; or
- o Are you going to purchase the property jointly, but as tenants-in-common in specified shares? This might well be appropriate if one partner is going to put in more towards the deposit than the other.

If one of you dies, that person's share would then devolve according to the terms of their Will (if they have one), or according to the rules of intestacy (if there is no Will)

▶ If you have children, the mother automatically has parental responsibility for them, but you need to ensure that the father is named on the birth certificate so that he has parental responsibility in the same way as the mother. The legal framework relating to children is to be found in The Children Act 1989.

▶ An unmarried father who is not named on the birth certificate may still enter into a Parental Responsibility Agreement with the mother, provided that she consents. If she does not, then the father will have to apply to the court for a Parental Responsibility Order under section 4 of The Children Act 1989

▶ Both parents are financially responsible for maintaining their children.

▶ If unmarried parents split up, then the legal framework covering the financial support for their children is regulated by the Children Act 1989, Schedule 1, and by the Child Support Act 1991

▶ For information about child support, see Child Support Options www.cmoptions.org

► There are many useful websites giving information about divorce, civil partnership dissolution and separation, for example National Family Mediation www.nfm.org.uk and Resolution, the organisation for family law solicitors www.resolution.org.uk

CHAPTER THIRTEEN

Difficult Times Together:
How To Cope When Things Go Wrong

How do you cope when things go wrong?

I t is vital to realise that every relationship goes through ups and downs – this is completely normal. No relationship will last through the years without challenging times along the way. There are certain things that can trigger serious problems in a relationship, like a mid-life crisis for one or both partners, the death of someone close, redundancy, financial problems, illness, addictions and so on. What matters most is how you handle such a crisis when it happens, and at the end of this chapter we give some useful tips to help you work out the best way forward.

Recognising a 'mid-life crisis'

The 'mid-life crisis' is likely to be experienced by those in their 40's and 50's, as it is then that the sense of one's own mortality starts to feel more imminent. The death of a parent, and maybe even of friends or siblings in one's own age group bring this even more starkly to the fore. This may give rise to thoughts such as 'is this all there is to life?' 'what have I achieved so far?' and 'what happened to all my dreams'?. This may prompt one to wish to explore experiences that have remained on the 'back-burner' until now, with an increased willingness to take risks, or even to 'have a fling' with someone else – things that might appear to others to be completely out of character for that person and wholly unexpected. Their partner may be left feeling as though 'someone flicked a switch and turned my husband/wife/ lover into a completely different person – I just don't know them anymore'. It can feel as though their partner is suffering from an illness for which there is apparently no cure.

Male and female experience of the mid-life crisis may be very different. It is not unusual to hear of middle-aged men joining a gym, buying new clothes, taking up new hobbies, befriending much younger women, and so on. Likewise, it is not unusual to see middle-aged women seek an emotional and physical 'make-over', have counselling to understand themselves, start to take more care over their appearance and begin to explore new relationships.

Loss of a child

The death of a child is likely to trigger huge changes in the dynamics of the parents' relationship. It is utterly devastating for both them and the resulting grief may leave them with no emotional reserves left for one another for a long time. They may learn to live with their loss but will never completely recover from it.

Story

Matt and Sue had been married for 20 years. Their daughter, Ann, tragically died at the age of 16 during a school trip. The couple received bereavement counselling and made every effort to come to terms with their loss. Sue found some solace in being able to talk to her female friends and a trained counsellor. However, Matt found it very difficult to talk about how he felt to Sue or to anyone else and he 'closed up' and withdrew into himself. Sue felt that he was shutting himself off from what had happened and compartmentalising the loss of their daughter from the rest of his life. To her this seemed as though he was in some way diminishing the importance of their daughter in his life. In fact, the truth was the opposite; closing this off in his mind was the only way Matt could bear to go on living without his daughter. Each of them had different ways of managing their feelings of loss and neither could really understand the other's viewpoint. Eventually their different ways of coping led to the breakdown of their marriage and they separated.

Loss of a parent

The death of a parent may result in huge changes for a couple, particularly where there was a close bond between the parent who has died and their child. However, even where the bereaved person was not particularly close to the parent concerned the death may bring to the surface emotions and issues that have remained buried in the past until that moment. This can act as a catalyst for a radical reassessment of how they have led their life so far, as a confirmation of their own mortality, and as a feeling that 'life is short'. This may lead to a questioning of life's purpose and a desire to overhaul and perhaps change the way they are living. One of the casualties of that reassessment may be the couple's relationship.

Redundancy

In Chapter 8 (Work) we have already talked about the pressures that the redundancy of one partner may bring for a couple, including a sudden loss of income, a lowering of their material standard of living, cancellation of holidays, a change in their social network, loss of self-worth, depression and so on. In many ways, the feelings experienced have parallels to those experienced during bereavement.

Financial problems

In Chapter 7 we looked at the way in which financial problems can place huge stress on a relationship and we suggested some ideas for managing these issues.

Physical illness and mental health problems

In Chapter 9 we considered the ways in which physical illness and mental health problems can lead to challenges for partners and we set out some suggested ways of seeking help and support.

Top tips for handling a crisis

If you do feel that things are starting to become more dif-ficult than they should be, it is important not to over-react at the first sign of trouble. Beware of taking irreversible steps before there has been a 'cooling off' period to give you time to think things through and to consider the consequences.

Try to talk through your concerns and anxieties with your partner first of all. Approach it as a joint prob-lem to which you wish to find a solution together. Try not simply to accuse them of doing something wrong, as this is likely to make them feel defensive and close down the conversation, and / or lead to an angry argu-ment between you that is unlikely to resolve anything. See the tips on communication in Chapter 4.

If you are able to talk to your partner and share some ideas about how you might work your way through the difficulties, follow it up with an agreed plan about the practical things you are going to try to do to change things. Leaving things as they are is unlikely to help, and may even make things worse.

If this does not resolve things, then talk to someone whose advice you trust. However, remember that family and friends may not always be the best people to help you in this situation as their first desire will be to protect you from hurt and harm, rather than to take a balanced view and give you wise advice about the future of your relationship.

Consider having some sessions of counselling for yourself, and / or jointly with your partner if you think that this might help. To find a suitable counsellor, speak to your family doctor, or seek recommendations from people who have already used their services. Don't leave it too late to seek help.

Remember these tips:

- ▶ Take time to calm down
- ▶ Don't rush into decisions
- ▶ Try to talk to your partner first of all
- ▶ Try to come up with a joint plan for things to do in order to improve the situation
- ▶ Consider joint counselling if your partner will agree to this. 'Relate' is a good place to start (www.relate.org.uk)
- ▶ Consider counselling for yourself (see 'Relate' above)

▶ Speak to someone you trust

▶ Seek medical advice if you feel depressed, anxious or unable to cope

▶ Look for a support group

▶ Seek legal advice if you feel that you need to protect yourself, your children and / or your financial position. 'Resolution' is a national organisation of family lawyers committed to non-confrontational divorce, separation and other family problems (www.resolution.org.uk).

▶ If it looks as though you are going to separate, consider family mediation as a way of reaching agreements with your partner about your finances and your children. National Family Mediation (www.nfm.org.uk) is a very useful source of information

▶ If you have suffered a bereavement, CRUSE (www.crusebereavementcare.org.uk) is a very useful source of help and support

CONCLUSION

We **hope** that you have found something useful in this book and have enjoyed reading it. It is intended to be something that you can 'dip into' as food for thought for yourself, to be used to stimulate ideas and discussion with others, or to be given to family and friends who may find it helpful.

It could make a great present!

RECOMMENDED READING

Don't Sweat the Small Stuff…and it's All Small Stuff - Richard Carlson (Hodder and Stoughton General Division,1998)

Men are from Mars, Women are from Venus - John Gray (Thorsons, 1993)

Mars and Venus, Together Forever - John Gray (Vermilion, 1996)

Mars and Venus, Starting Over - John Gray (Vermilion, 1998)

The Road Less Travelled - M. Scott Peck (Rider, 1997)

You just don't Understand. Men and Women in Conversation - Deborah Tannen (Virago Press 1992)

Marriage and Morals Bertrand Russell (1985), (Routledge Classics, 2009)

Type Talk: The 16 Personality Types- Otto Kroeger and Janet M. Thuesen (Paperback - 31 Dec 1989)

Families and How to Survive Them - John Cleese and Robin Skinner (Mandarin, 1983)

Brilliant Relationships - Annie Lionett (Sheldon Press, 2008)

Conscious Relationships - Lori S Rubenstein (Dare to Transcend Series, 2006)

Love Life - Janet Reibstein (Fourth Estate Limited, 1997) (A Channel Four Publication)

Why Men Lie, and Women Cry - Allan and Barbara Pease (Orion, 2002)

Making Relationships Work - Alison Waines (Sheldon Press)

The Rules of Love - Richard Templar (Pearson Education)

Brilliant Relationships - Annie Lionnet (Pearson Education)

For Better or for Worse: The Science of a Good Marriage - Tara Parker-Pope (Random House)

COMPLIMENTARY
DIGITAL EDITION

A complimentary digital edition
is included with this book.

To download your epub, mobi & PDF ver-
sions of this book, please navigate to:

www.commonsenseforcouples.com/ebook

When prompted for a password enter the
following:

C0mM0nS£ns£

VISIT OUR WEBSITE

For more relationship tips, visit our website at

www.commonsenseforcouples.com

THANKS FOR READING!

Remember at <u>www.dibbooks.com</u> you can:

Join our newsletter

Browse our catalogue

Read our free Story of the Week

Thank you for picking up one of our titles!